HAL LEONARD
GUITAR METHOD
Supplement to Any Guitar Method

EASY SOLO GUITAR PIECES
15 Popular Songs Arranged for Beginning Chord Melody Style in Standard Notation

T0085615

ISBN 978-1-4768-7563-7

HAL•LEONARD®
CORPORATION
7777 W. BLUEMOUND RD. P.O. BOX 13819 MILWAUKEE, WI 53213

Visit Hal Leonard Online at
www.halleonard.com

Best of My Love

Words and Music by John David Souther,
Don Henley and Glenn Frey

Verse
Slow ♩ = 72

1. Ev - er - y night ___ I'm ly - in' in bed ___ hold - in' you close ___ to my
2., 3. *See additional lyrics*
let ring throughout

dreams; ___ think - in' a - bout ___ all the things that we said and

com - in' a - part ___ at the seams. ___ We tried to talk it o -

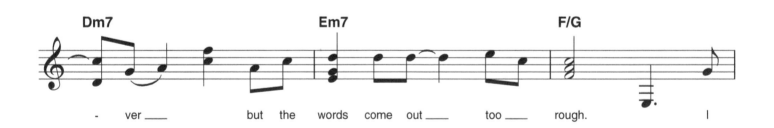

- ver ___ but the words come out ___ too ___ rough. I

know you were try - in' to give me the best ___ of your love.

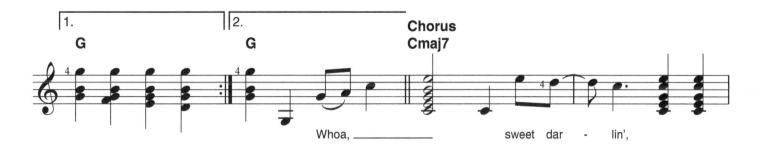

Whoa, _____ sweet dar - lin',

you get the best of my love. __ Whoa, _____ sweet dar -

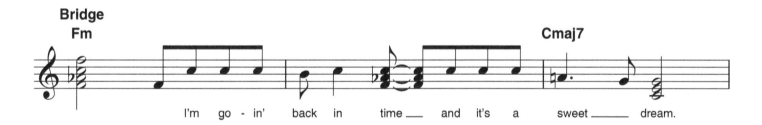

- lin', you get the best of my __ love.

I'm go - in' back in time __ and it's a sweet _____ dream.

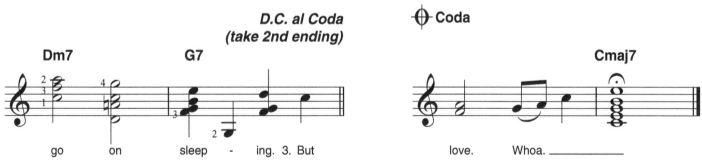

It was a qui - et night, __ and I would be al - right __ if I could

go on sleep - ing. 3. But

love. Whoa. _____

Additional Lyrics

2. Beautiful faces an' loud empty places,
   Look at the way that we live;
   Wastin' our time on cheap talk and wine,
   Left us so little to give.
   That same old crowd was like a cold dark cloud
   That we could never rise above.
   But here in my heart
   I give you the best of my love.

3. But ev'ry morning I wake up and worry
   What's gonna happen today.
   You see it your way and I'll see it mine
   But we both see it slippin' away.
   You know we always had each other, baby,
   I guess that wasn't enough;
   Oh, oh, but here in my heart
   I give you the best of my love.

Bridge Over Troubled Water

Words and Music by Paul Simon

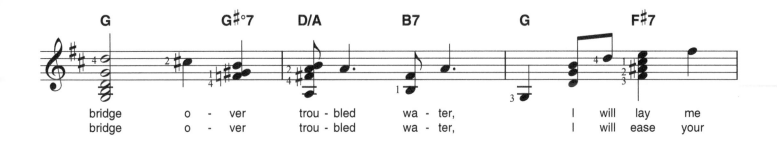

bridge   o - ver   trou - bled   wa - ter,   I will lay me
bridge   o - ver   trou - bled   wa - ter,   I will ease your

To Coda ⊕

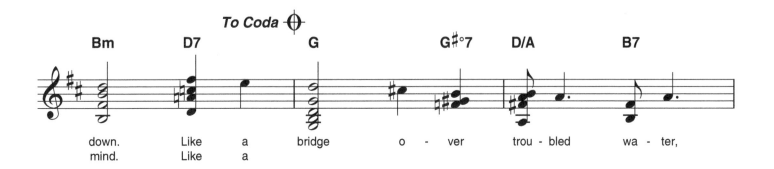

down.   Like   a   bridge   o - ver   trou - bled   wa - ter,
mind.   Like   a

I will lay me down.

D.S. al Coda

2. Sail   on

⊕ **Coda**

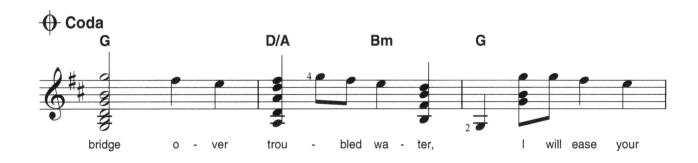

bridge   o - ver   trou - bled wa - ter,   I will ease your

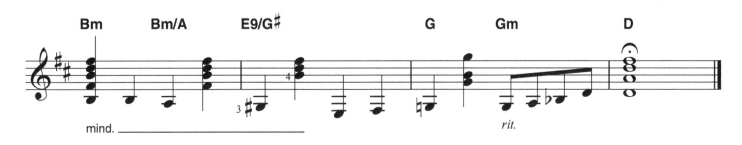

mind. _____   *rit.*

Crazy

Words and Music by Willie Nelson

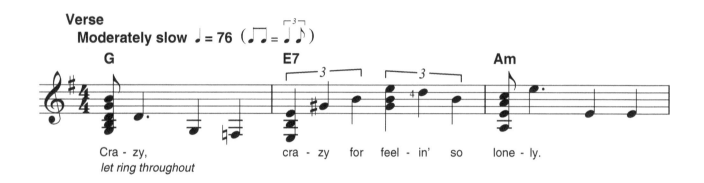

A♯°7 G7/B **Bridge** C C♯°7

Wor - ry, why do I let my - self

G A7

wor - ry, won - d'rin'

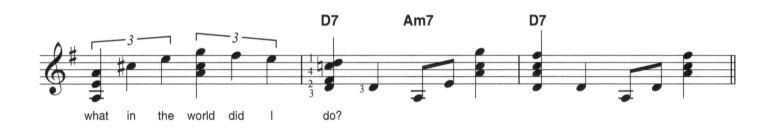

D7 Am7 D7

what in the world did I do?

Outro-Verse

G E7 Am

Cra - zy, for think - ing that my love could hold you,

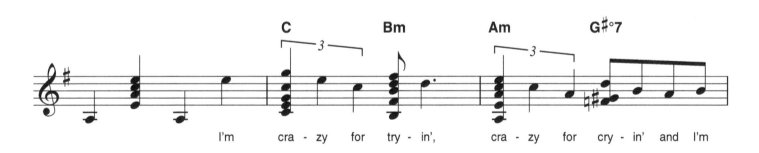

C Bm Am G♯°7

I'm cra - zy for try - in', cra - zy for cry - in' and I'm

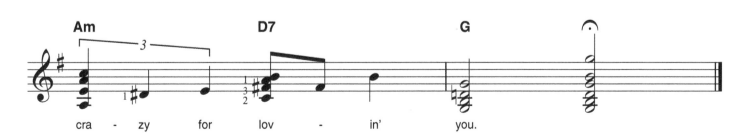

Am D7 G

cra - zy for lov - in' you.

7

Good Vibrations

Words and Music by Brian Wilson
and Mike Love

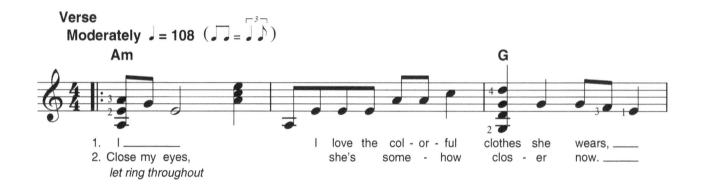

1. I _____ I love the col - or - ful clothes she wears, ____
2. Close my eyes, she's some - how clos - er now. ____

let ring throughout

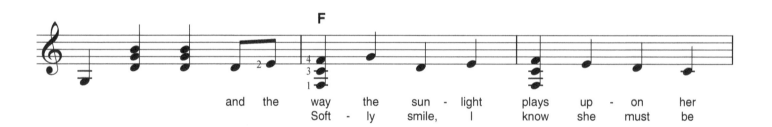

and the way the sun - light plays up - on her
Soft - ly smile, I know she must be

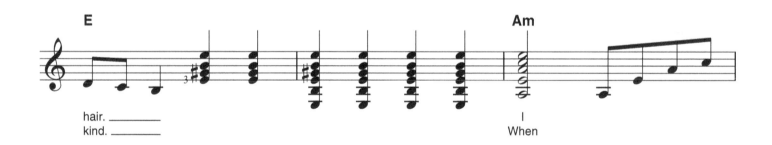

hair. _____ I
kind. _____ When

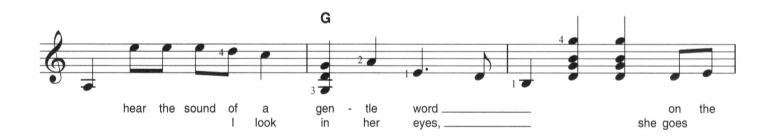

hear the sound of a gen - tle word _____ on the
I look in her eyes, _____ she goes

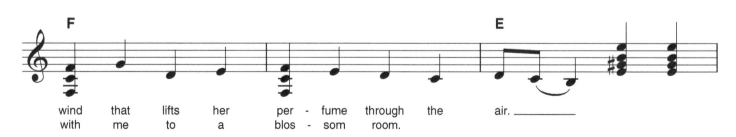

wind that lifts her per - fume through the air. _____
with me to a blos - som room.

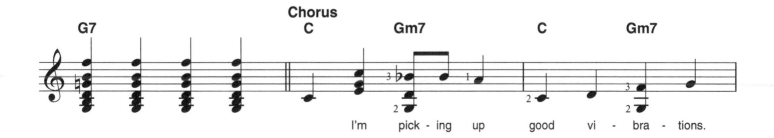

Chorus

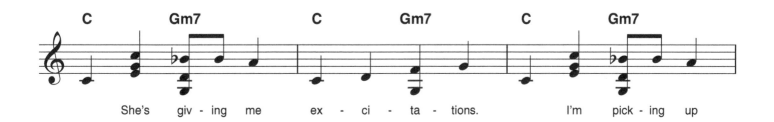

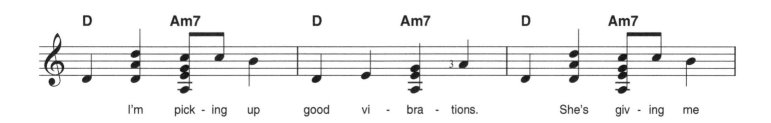

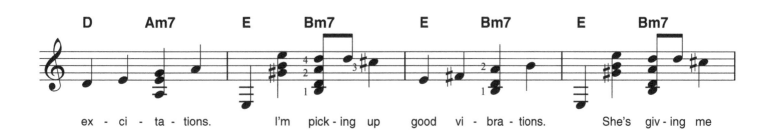

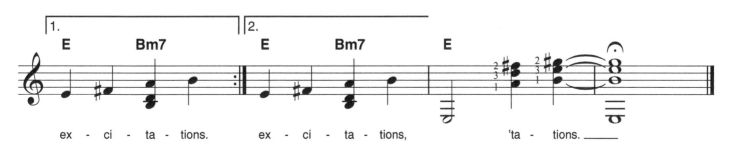

I Just Called to Say I Love You

Words and Music by Stevie Wonder

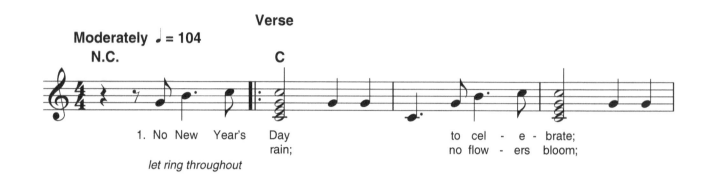

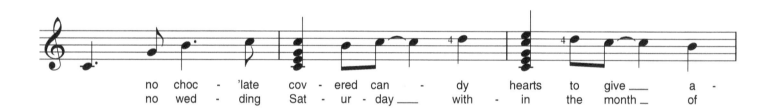

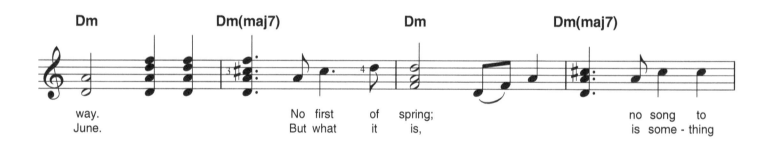

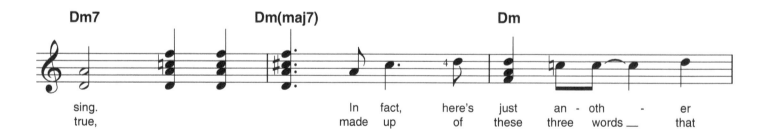

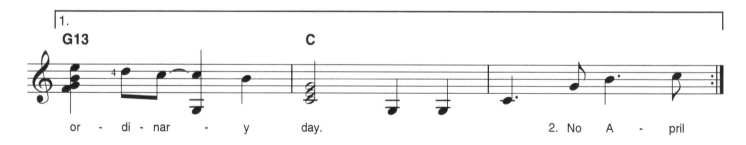

I must say ___ to you.   I just called ___   to say ___

___   I love ___ you.   I just called ___

___   to say ___ how much ___ I care.   I just called ___

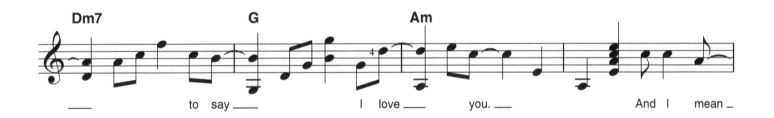

___   to say ___   I love ___ you. ___   And I mean ___

___ it from ___ the bot - tom of ___ my heart,   of   my

heart,   of   my   heart.

In My Life

Words and Music by John Lennon
and Paul McCartney

Intro
Moderately slow ♩ = 84

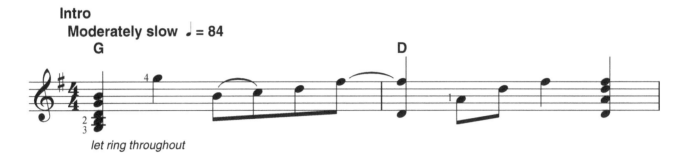

let ring throughout

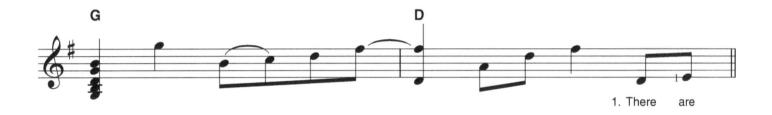

1. There are

Verse

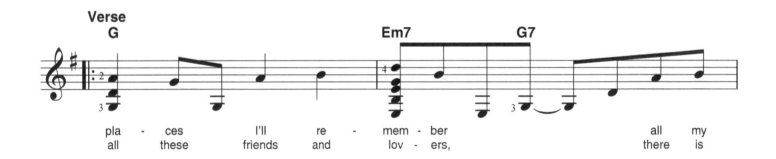

pla - ces   I'll   re -   mem - ber   all   my
all these   friends   and   lov - ers,   there is

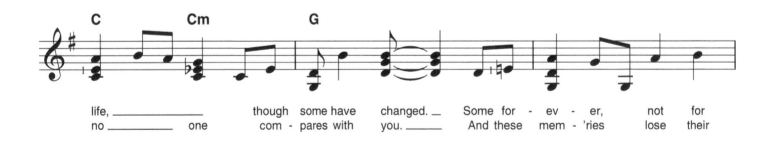

life, _____   though some have   changed. _   Some for - ev - er,   not   for
no ____ one   com - pares with   you. ____   And these mem - 'ries   lose   their

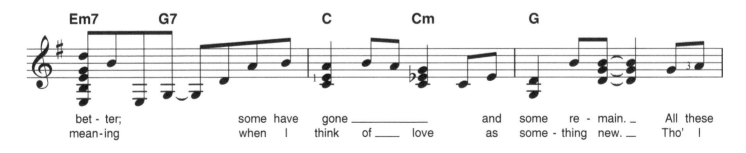

bet - ter;   some have   gone ___   and some re - main. _   All these
mean - ing   when   I   think   of ___ love   as   some - thing new. _ Tho' I

12

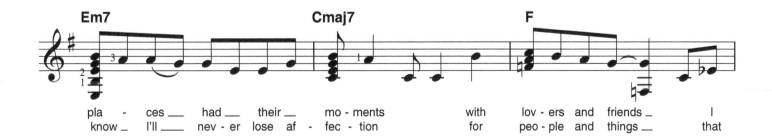

pla - ces __ had __ their __ mo - ments   with   lov - ers and friends __   I
know __ I'll __ nev - er lose af - fec - tion   for   peo - ple and things __   that

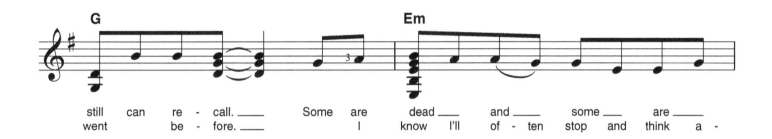

still   can   re - call. ____   Some   are   dead __ and ____ some __   are ____
went   be - fore. ____   I   know I'll   of - ten stop   and   think a -

liv - ing,   in   my _____ life   I've   loved   them   all. ____
bout them,   in   my _____ life   I   love   you   more. __

2. But of   In

Outro

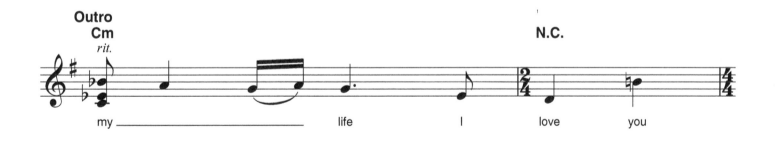

my _____   life   I   love   you

A tempo

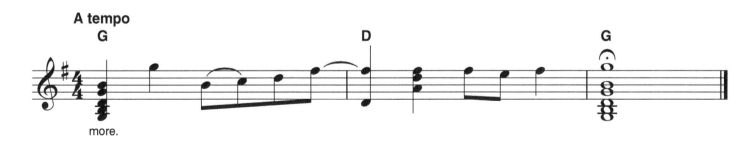

more.

Just the Way You Are

Words and Music by Billy Joel

Verse
Moderately slow ♩ = 88

1. Don't go chang-ing to try and
   would not leave you in times of
3. *See additional lyrics*

let ring throughout

please me; you nev-er let me down ___ be-
trou-ble; we nev-er could have come ___ this

fore. Don't im-ag - ine
far. I took the good times;

you're too fa - mil - iar and I ___ don't
I'll take the bad times.

see you an-y-more. ___

2. I I'll take ___ you

just the way ___ you are. ___

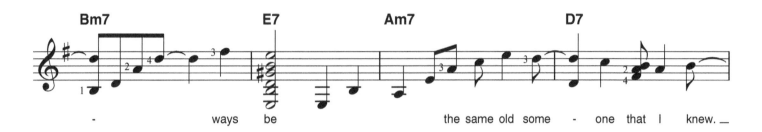

I need to know that you ___ will al -

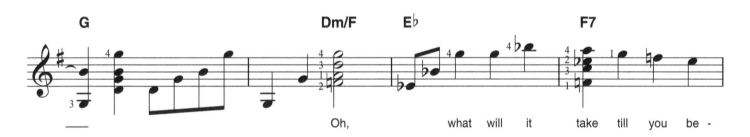

- ways be the same old some - one that I knew. ___

Oh, what will it take till you be -

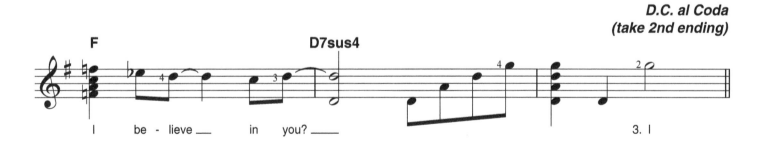

lieve in me the way that

D.C. al Coda
(take 2nd ending)

I be - lieve ___ in you? ___ 3. I

Coda

Additional Lyrics

3. I said I love you, and that's forever,
And this I promise from the heart. Mm.
I could not love you any better,
I love you just the way you are.

Lean on Me

Words and Music by Bill Withers

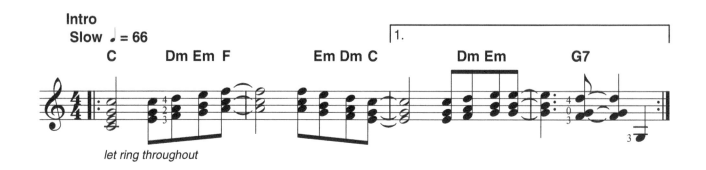

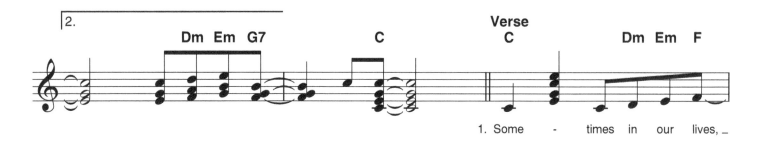

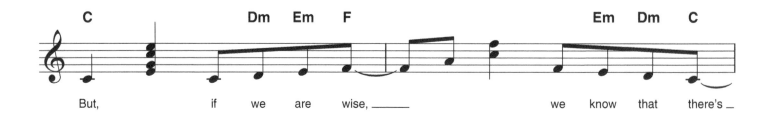

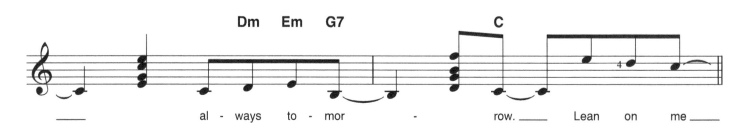

Chorus

when you're not strong, _____ and I'll be your friend, _

___ I'll help you car - ry on, _____ for it won't be long _

_____ 'til I'm gon - na need ___ some - bod - y to lean _____ on. _

Verse

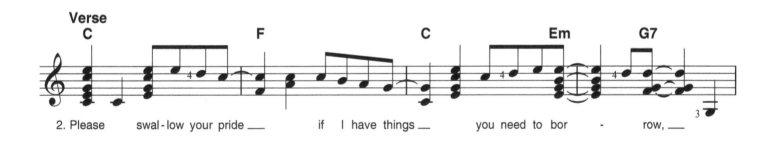

2. Please swal - low your pride ___ if I have things ___ you need to bor - row, ___

for no one can fill _____ all of your needs ___ that you won't let _____ show. _ You just

Outro

call ___ me, _ call ___ me, _ call ___ me. _

My Favorite Things

from THE SOUND OF MUSIC

Lyrics by Oscar Hammerstein II
Music by Richard Rodgers

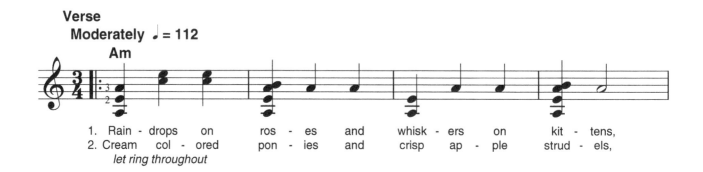

Verse
Moderately ♩ = 112

Am

1. Rain - drops on ros - es and whisk - ers on kit - tens,
2. Cream col - ored pon - ies and crisp ap - ple strud - els,

let ring throughout

Fmaj7

bright cop - per ket - tles and warm wool - en mit - tens;
door - bells and sleigh - bells and schnitz - el with noo - dles;

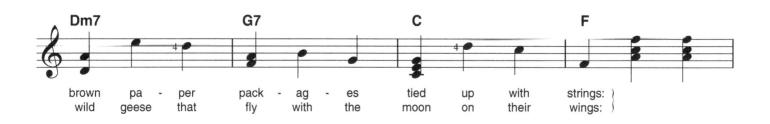

Dm7   **G7**   **C**   **F**

brown pa - per pack - ag - es tied up with strings: }
wild geese that fly with the moon on their wings: }

C   **F**   **1.**   **Dm**   **E7**

These are a few of my fa - vor - ite things.

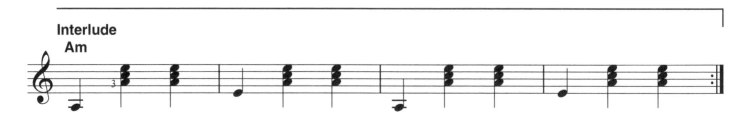

Interlude
Am

fa - vor - ite things. When the dog bites,

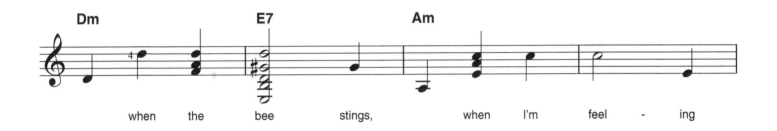

when the bee stings, when I'm feel - ing

sad, I sim - ply re - mem - ber my

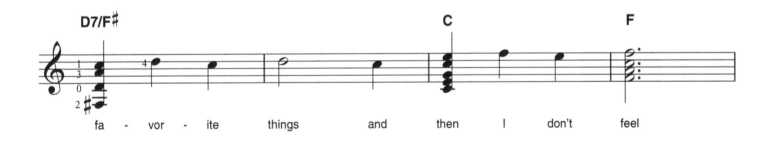

fa - vor - ite things and then I don't feel

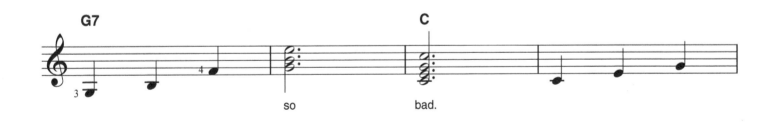

so bad.

People Get Ready

Words and Music by Curtis Mayfield

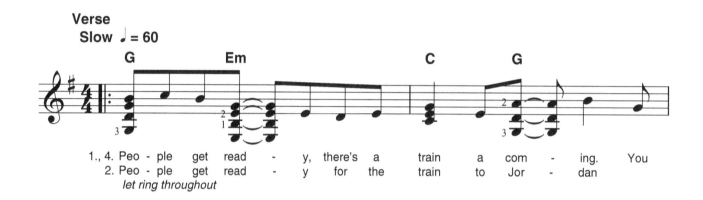

1., 4. Peo - ple get read - y, there's a train a com - ing. You
2. Peo - ple get read - y for the train to Jor - dan

let ring throughout

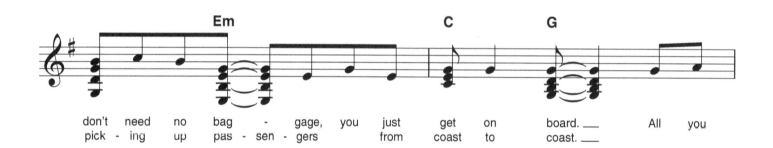

don't need no bag - gage, you just get on board. ___ All you
pick - ing up pas - sen - gers just from coast to coast. ___

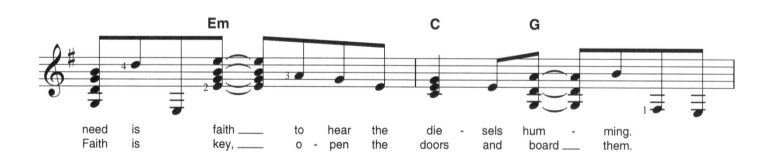

need is faith ___ to hear the die - sels hum - ming.
Faith is key, ___ o - pen the doors and board ___ them.

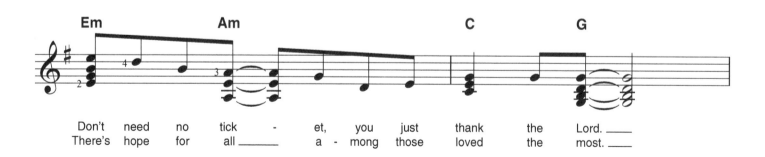

Don't need no tick - et, you just thank the Lord. ___
There's hope for all ___ a - mong those loved the most. ___

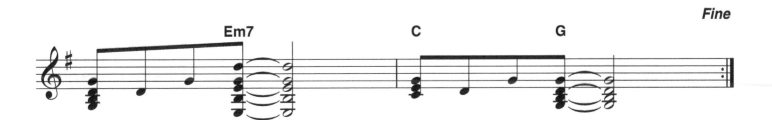

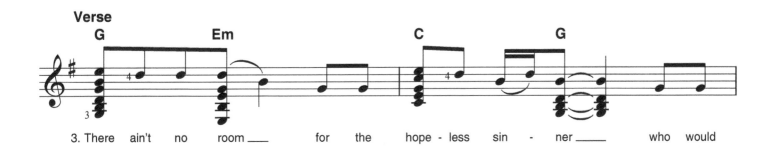

Verse

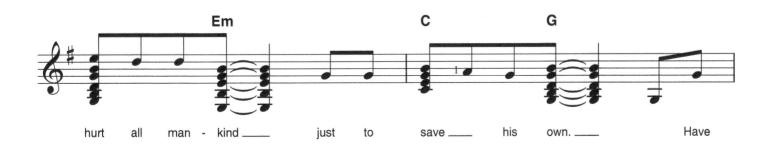

3. There ain't no room ____ for the hope-less sin - ner ____ who would

hurt all man - kind ____ just to save ____ his own. ____ Have

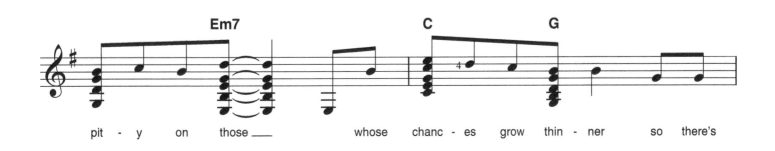

pit - y on those ____ whose chanc - es grow thin - ner so there's

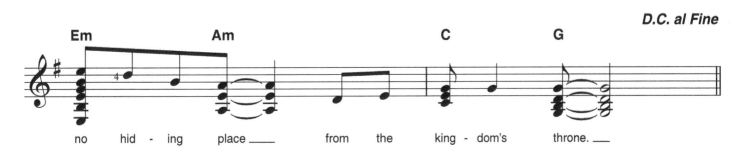

no hid - ing place ____ from the king - dom's throne. ____

The Pink Panther

from THE PINK PANTHER

By Henry Mancini

A

Moderately slow ♩ = 92

What a Wonderful World

Words and Music by George David Weiss
and Bob Thiele

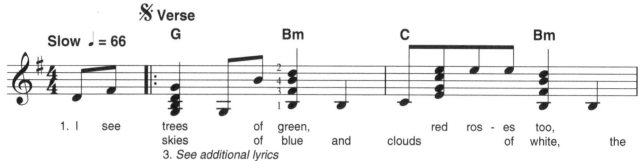

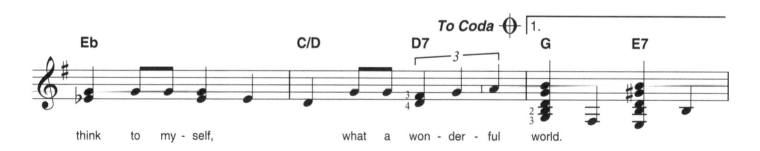

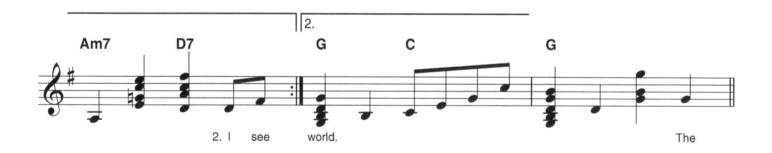

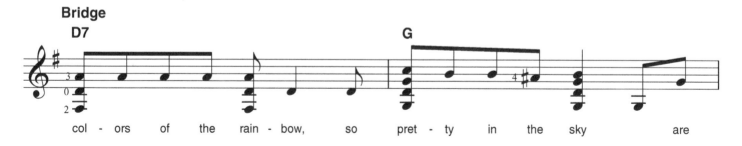

al - so on the fac - es of peo - ple go - in' by. I hear

friends shak - in' hands, say - in' "How do you do?"

D.S. al Coda

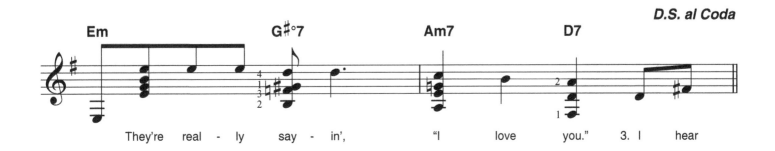

They're real - ly say - in', "I love you." 3. I hear

world. _____ Yes, I think to my - self,

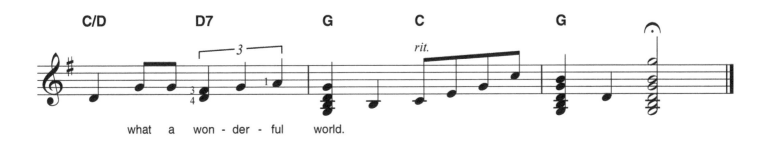

what a won - der - ful world.

Additional Lyrics

3. I hear babies cry. I watch them grow.
They'll learn much more than I'll ever know,
And I think to myself, what a wonderful world.

When You Wish Upon a Star

Words by Ned Washington
Music by Leigh Harline

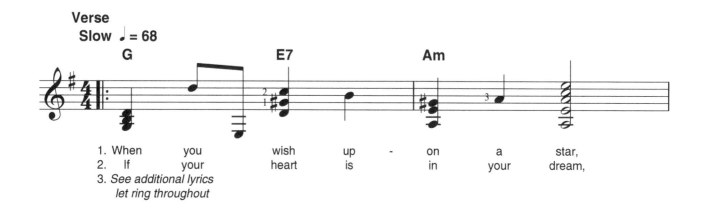

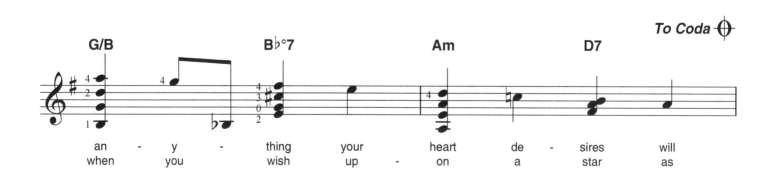

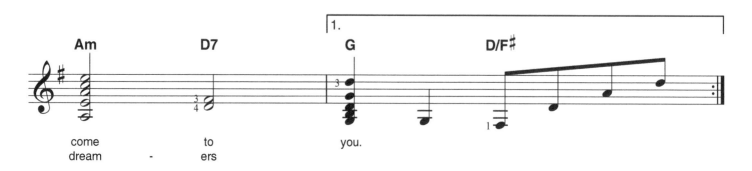

do.

Fate is

kind,

she brings to

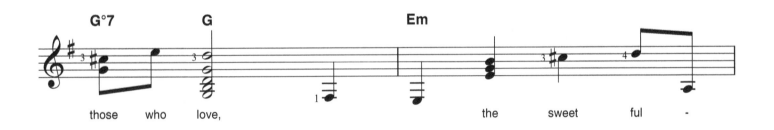

those who love,

the sweet ful -

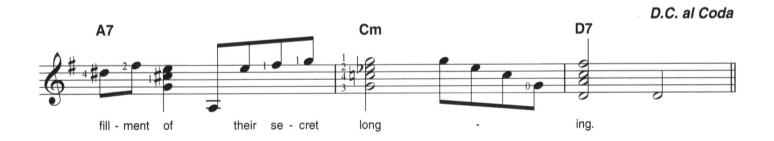

D.C. al Coda

fill - ment of

their se - cret long - ing.

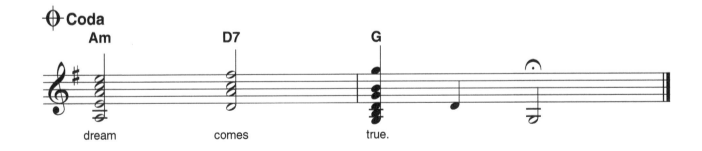

Coda

dream

comes

true.

Additional Lyrics

3. Like a bolt out of the blue,
Fate steps in and sees you thru.
When you wish upon a star,
Your dream comes true.

You Are So Beautiful

Words and Music by Billy Preston
and Bruce Fisher

Intro
Slow ♩ = 56

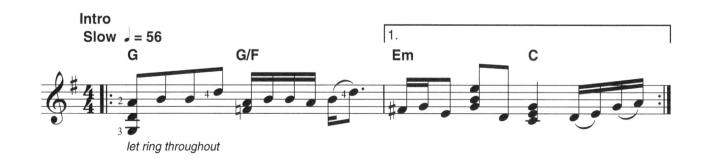

let ring throughout

1., 2. You are so beau-ti-ful ____

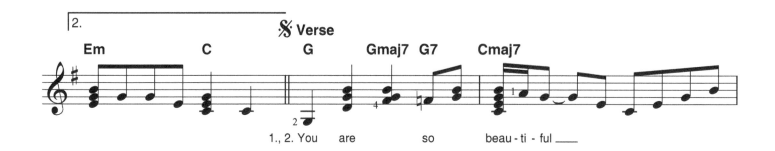

to me. You are so

beau-ti-ful ____ to me, can't you

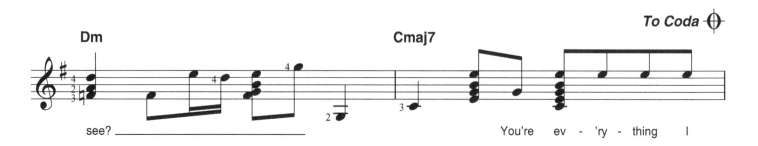

see? _____ You're ev-'ry-thing I

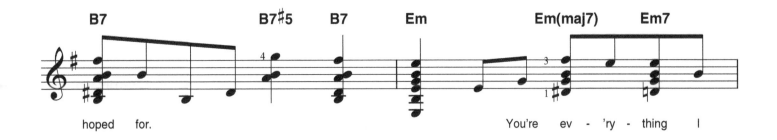

hoped for.   You're ev - 'ry - thing I

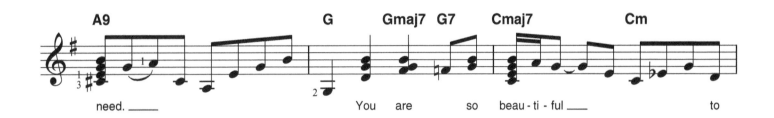

need. _____   You are so beau - ti - ful _____ to

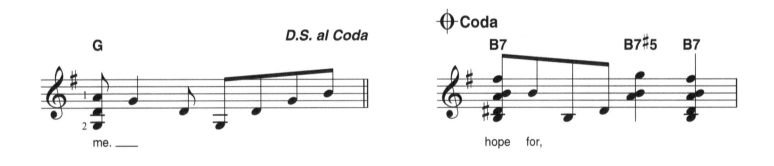

D.S. al Coda

Coda

me. _____   hope for,

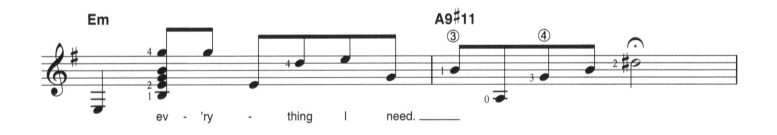

ev - 'ry - thing I need. _____

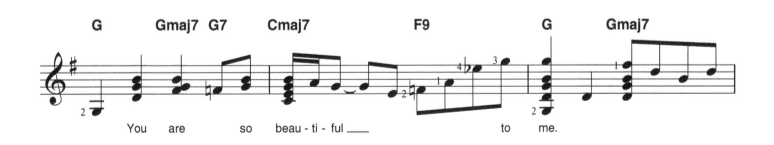

You are so beau - ti - ful _____ to me.

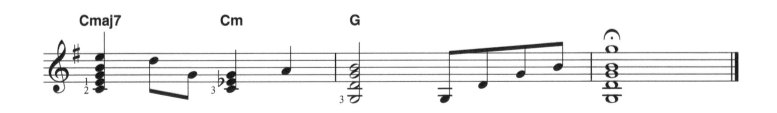

Your Song

Words and Music by Elton John
and Bernie Taupin

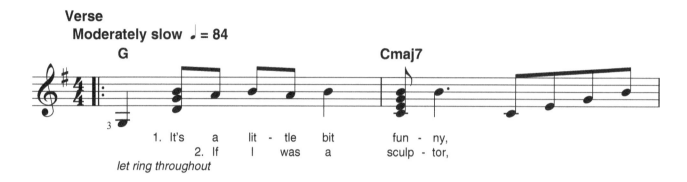

Verse
Moderately slow ♩ = 84

let ring throughout

1. It's a lit - tle bit fun - ny,
2. If I was a sculp - tor,

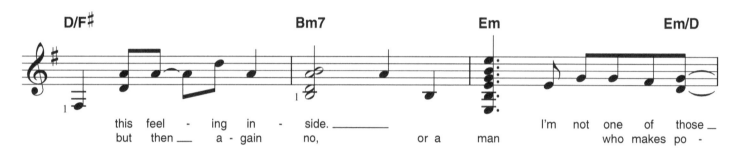

this feel - ing in - side. _____
but then _____ a - gain no, or a man

I'm not one of those _____
who makes po -

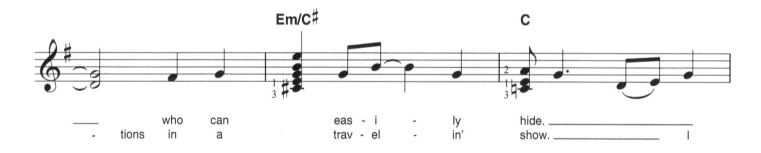

_____ who can eas - i - ly hide. _____
- tions in a trav - el - in' show. _____ I

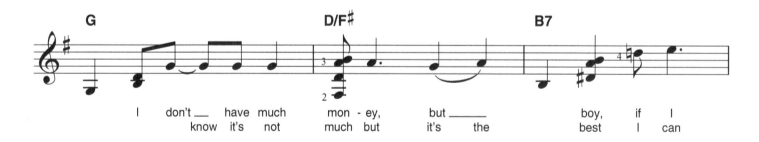

I don't _____ have much mon - ey, but _____ boy, if I
know it's not much but it's the best I can

did, _____
do. _____

I'd buy _____ a big house where _____
My gift _____ is my song and _____

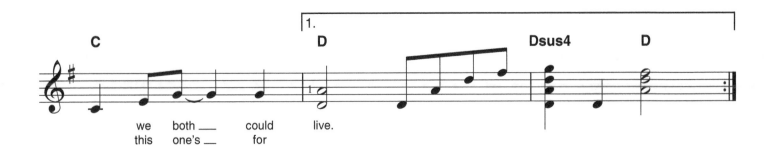

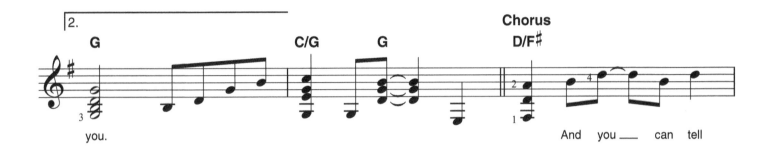

we both __ could   live.
this one's __ for

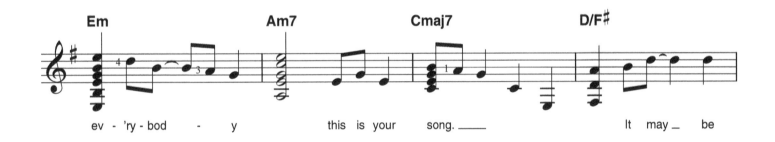

you.   And you __ can tell

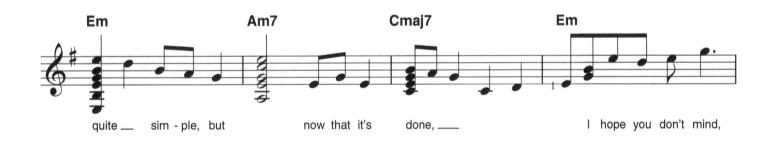

ev - 'ry-bod - y   this is your   song. ____   It may __ be

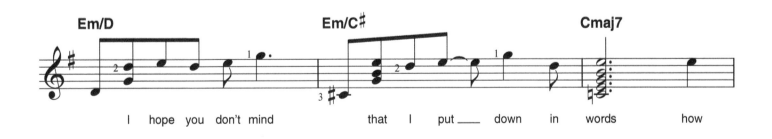

quite __ sim - ple, but   now that it's   done, ____   I hope you don't mind,

I hope you don't mind   that I put __ down in words   how

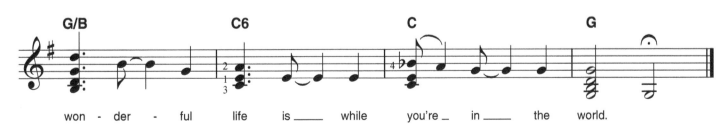

won - der - ful life is ____ while   you're __ in ____ the world.

HAL LEONARD GUITAR METHOD

METHOD BOOKS, SONGBOOKS AND REFERENCE BOOKS

THE HAL LEONARD GUITAR METHOD is designed for anyone just learning to play acoustic or electric guitar. It is based on years of teaching guitar students of all ages, and it also reflects some of the best guitar teaching ideas from around the world. This comprehensive method includes: A learning sequence carefully paced with clear instructions; popular songs which increase the incentive to learn to play; versatility – can be used as self-instruction or with a teacher; audio accompaniments so that students have fun and sound great while practicing.

BOOK 1
00699010	Book Only	$8.99
00699027	Book/Online Audio	$12.99
00697341	Book/Online Audio + DVD	$24.99
00697318	DVD Only	$19.99
00155480	Deluxe Beginner Edition (Book, CD, DVD, Online Audio/ Video & Chord Poster)	$19.99

COMPLETE (BOOKS 1, 2 & 3)
00699040	Book Only	$16.99
00697342	Book/Online Audio	$24.99

BOOK 2
00699020	Book Only	$8.99
00697313	Book/Online Audio	$12.99

BOOK 3
00699030	Book Only	$8.99
00697316	Book/Online Audio	$12.99

Prices, contents and availability subject to change without notice.

STYLISTIC METHODS

ACOUSTIC GUITAR
00697347	Method Book/Online Audio	$17.99
00237969	Songbook/Online Audio	$16.99

BLUEGRASS GUITAR
00697405	Method Book/Online Audio	$16.99

BLUES GUITAR
00697326	Method Book/Online Audio (9" x 12")	$16.99
00697344	Method Book/Online Audio (6" x 9")	$15.99
00697385	Songbook/Online Audio (9" x 12")	$14.99
00248636	Kids Method Book/Online Audio	$12.99

BRAZILIAN GUITAR
00697415	Method Book/Online Audio	$17.99

CHRISTIAN GUITAR
00695947	Method Book/Online Audio	$16.99
00697408	Songbook/CD Pack	$14.99

CLASSICAL GUITAR
00697376	Method Book/Online Audio	$15.99

COUNTRY GUITAR
00697337	Method Book/Online Audio	$22.99
00697400	Songbook/Online Audio	$19.99

FINGERSTYLE GUITAR
00697378	Method Book/Online Audio	$21.99
00697432	Songbook/Online Audio	$16.99

FLAMENCO GUITAR
00697363	Method Book/Online Audio	$15.99

FOLK GUITAR
00697414	Method Book/Online Audio	$16.99

JAZZ GUITAR
00695359	Book/Online Audio	$22.99
00697386	Songbook/Online Audio	$15.99

JAZZ-ROCK FUSION
00697387	Book/Online Audio	$24.99

R&B GUITAR
00697356	Book/Online Audio	$19.99
00697433	Songbook/CD Pack	$14.99

ROCK GUITAR
00697319	Book/Online Audio	$16.99
00697383	Songbook/Online Audio	$16.99

ROCKABILLY GUITAR
00697407	Book/Online Audio	$16.99

OTHER METHOD BOOKS

BARITONE GUITAR METHOD
00242055	Book/Online Audio	$12.99

GUITAR FOR KIDS
00865003	Method Book 1/Online Audio	$12.99
00697402	Songbook/Online Audio	$9.99
00128437	Method Book 2/Online Audio	$12.99

MUSIC THEORY FOR GUITARISTS
00695790	Book/Online Audio	$19.99

TENOR GUITAR METHOD
00148330	Book/Online Audio	$12.99

12-STRING GUITAR METHOD
00249528	Book/Online Audio	$19.99

METHOD SUPPLEMENTS

ARPEGGIO FINDER
00697352	6" x 9" Edition	$6.99
00697351	9" x 12" Edition	$9.99

BARRE CHORDS
00697406	Book/Online Audio	$14.99

CHORD, SCALE & ARPEGGIO FINDER
00697410	Book Only	$19.99

GUITAR TECHNIQUES
00697389	Book/Online Audio	$16.99

INCREDIBLE CHORD FINDER
00697200	6" x 9" Edition	$7.99
00697208	9" x 12" Edition	$7.99

INCREDIBLE SCALE FINDER
00695568	6" x 9" Edition	$9.99
00695490	9" x 12" Edition	$9.99

LEAD LICKS
00697345	Book/Online Audio	$10.99

RHYTHM RIFFS
00697346	Book/Online Audio	$14.99

SONGBOOKS

CLASSICAL GUITAR PIECES
00697388	Book/Online Audio	$9.99

EASY POP MELODIES
00697281	Book Only	$7.99
00697440	Book/Online Audio	$14.99

(MORE) EASY POP MELODIES
00697280	Book Only	$6.99
00697269	Book/Online Audio	$14.99

(EVEN MORE) EASY POP MELODIES
00699154	Book Only	$6.99
00697439	Book/Online Audio	$14.99

EASY POP RHYTHMS
00697336	Book Only	$7.99
00697441	Book/Online Audio	$14.99

(MORE) EASY POP RHYTHMS
00697338	Book Only	$7.99
00697322	Book/Online Audio	$14.99

(EVEN MORE) EASY POP RHYTHMS
00697340	Book Only	$7.99
00697323	Book/Online Audio	$14.99

EASY POP CHRISTMAS MELODIES
00697417	Book Only	$9.99
00697416	Book/Online Audio	$14.99

EASY POP CHRISTMAS RHYTHMS
00278177	Book Only	$6.99
00278175	Book/Online Audio	$14.99

EASY SOLO GUITAR PIECES
00110407	Book Only	$9.99

REFERENCE

GUITAR PRACTICE PLANNER
00697401	Book Only	$5.99

GUITAR SETUP & MAINTENANCE
00697427	6" x 9" Edition	$14.99
00697421	9" x 12" Edition	$12.99

For more info, songlists, or to purchase these and more books from your favorite music retailer, go to

halleonard.com

HAL•LEONARD®